From my heart to yours

Mirza Afshan

ISBN
Paperback 979-8-89744-996-5
Hardcase 979-8-89984-259-7

Prologue

I'm Afshan, and life has taken me through more than I ever imagined. Last July, I had a severe mental breakdown- one that felt like everything was collapsing all at once. Since then, I've been on SSRIs and Clonazepam, trying to piece myself back together. In those dark months, I turned to self-help books and poetry, searching for understanding. But what truly saved me was writing.

Writing helped me make sense of what I was feeling, to see myself clearly, to process emotions I didn't even realize I had. And when I revisited my own poetry, I saw it; this wasn't sudden. It had been building for years. I had felt alone, misjudged, unheard. And I couldn't help but wonder: if I had come across a writer who had laid bare their struggles with rawness and honesty, maybe I wouldn't have felt so isolated. Maybe I could have seen myself in their words. Maybe; just maybe; the breakdown wouldn't have hit as hard.

That's why this book exists. Every poem, every excerpt, is a piece of my heart extended to you, so you know you are seen. This is an unfiltered chronicle of my journey from 18 to 24. Unlike many poetry books that stem from fiction, this one is deeply personal; drawn from real experiences of independence, loss, self-discovery, and the unpredictable nature of life.

I completed my MBBS abroad; not just for a degree, but as an escape from home. I was a rebel, searching for independence. But what I learned in those years, beyond medicine, shaped this book. It was never meant to be published; it was just my way of making sense of things. But over time, I realized something; the messy, confusing, untamed, and real stories deserve to be shared.

I want you, the reader, to find something in these words. To know that you're not alone in the chaos, that there are others still figuring things out, still holding on. And that it's okay.

Blending poetry and illustration, this book moves between the deeply personal and the abstract, allowing you to find your own meaning in its words. I hope it speaks to you the way writing it spoke to me.

Note: The whole book is divided into different phases annotated by different fonts.

August 2019

Never be a girl, you won't know the way,
In this world where rules are set astray.
Never be free of fear,
For your own braid might bring you near.

Always stay active, keep moving through,
Boldness, a choice—only for the few.
Act with grace, and modesty wear,
While others revel in cruelty, unaware.

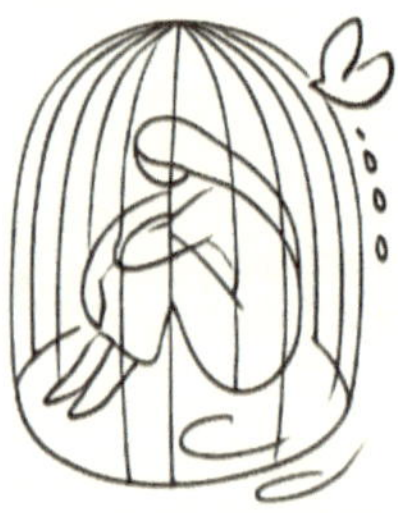

Cry in silence, let no one see,
For when you do, who will believe thee?
Boldness, a shield that should not show,
Endure, conceal, and let nothing grow.

No right to anger, no room to weep,
When others strike, your soul must keep.
Tolerate the storms, the pain, the rage,
And turn the page without a word to say.

Afraid that I won't be able to gather my
broken pieces

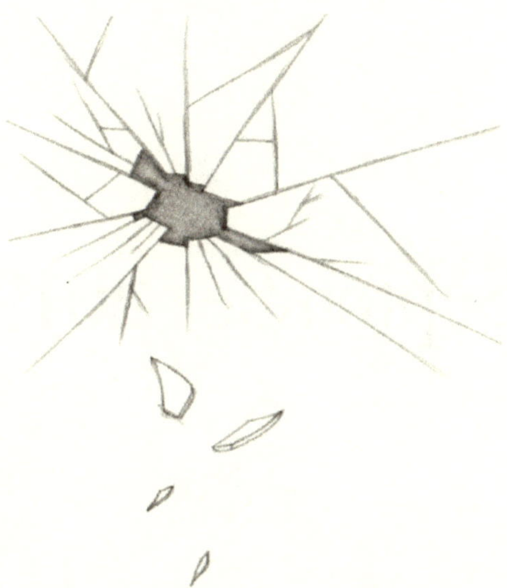

Won but somehow managed to lose myself

September 2019

I guess it makes sense somehow
The pain, the agony, and the false vow

I guess it was never meant to be
Happy ending that's not for me

Suffer, the world screamed
Death would knock, it seemed

But I did no crime
Why? Would things stop the time

I guess I'll keep mum
The feels are all numb

To that command of wrong
My life is not my own

Took me long to find contentment
But now, it's just resentment

Worse? Yes it is more
Pain? Keeps getting sore

Unfortunate and unexpected
Turns are all awaited

Sigh and sorrow
Don't wannna wake up tomorrow

I guess I should keep mum like I've always been Doing
So that I won't be snubbed and life gets soothing

Following the command of wrong
I guess a girl's life is never her own

November 2019

The sky, once painted in hues of blue,
Now wears a pallor, its colors few.
The grass that stretched with vibrant grace,
Now bends, its green a shadowed trace.

A soul once sweet, now sour with time,
Where joy once danced, now aches climb.
A smile I wear, to mask the cry,
Yet in the quiet, I wonder why.

I had a purpose, now it's gone,
The tethered threads unravel, undone.
The more I cling, the faster they fade,
Hope doesn't heal—it keeps me chained.

Lips once kissed by life's soft hue,
Now pale and worn, with nothing new.
Pushed into deeds I never sought,
My mind, a labyrinth, deeply fraught.

Perhaps it's fate, perhaps it's right,
That joy escapes my grasping sight.
They call it sorrow, call it pain,
But flames don't burn beneath this rain.
To rise once more, to start anew,
Takes more than strength—it takes the truth.
They tell me it's all in my mind,
Yet shadows linger, unconfined.

I wear my courage like a mask,
A front for those too scared to ask.
But what of the self that stays unseen,
The weary heart, the in-between?
Hope adorns me, stitched with lies,
A smile that fools the watching eyes.
Perhaps tomorrow will bring a spark,
Yet armor shields a hollow heart.

April 2020

The wave crashes against your weary soul, eroding the edges of your resolve. Tired of your Botox smile, you long to break down—but you are powerless. It's not that you're holding it back anymore; it's that you've buried it for so long beneath that plastic grin that it has dissolved into the emptiness within you.

A black hole festers deep inside, feeding on your emotions, consuming them until nothing remains. You feel its presence, a void gnawing at the edges of your being, yet its origins remain elusive—rooted somewhere beyond reach, deep within.

You grasp at straws, but the truth is undeniable: you have crossed the point of no return. And so, you wait. You always do. This wave is not the first, nor will it be the last.
Yet, no matter how many times it pulls you under, it always feels like the first—because you never truly grow used to emptiness, even when it has become a part of you.

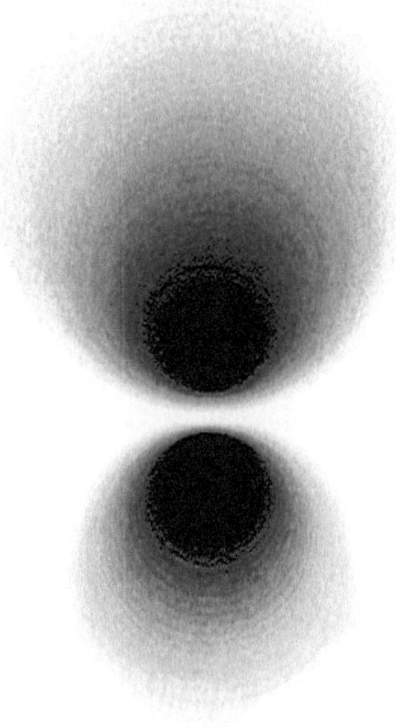

May 2020

If you ever find yourself entangled in the belief that it is the end of the world, know this: it is not (not yet, though 2020 has hardly painted an optimistic picture, to say the least). We all possess a reason to endure, no matter how minuscule it may appear—the warmth in the smile of your parents, or more weighty truths such as: YOU HAVE A LIFE WAITING TO BE LIVED!!! (And one filled with boundless potential). We are but a collective of beings encumbered by complexities.

This quarantine has forced us into an unavoidable reckoning with ourselves, a confrontation with the self we've long evaded by fleeing from our struggles. Yet, in this enforced stillness, we have nowhere to hide. Perhaps now is the time to introspect. To truly perceive who we are, to delve into the depths of our being, and to embark on the journey of self-betterment.

Let go of the distractions of others' existences. Each of us fights our own battles, engaging with them according to our unique capabilities. Cast aside the denial! It is time to face your fears, your limitations, your setbacks—just face yourself. It will get better.

June 2020

We ought to cling on to any 'delight/good' that life offers because (sometimes) we are so deprived of all the joy and affection that we cannot let it pass by, even when we know it's not right/is delusional. We jump all fences (of reality) just to grasp that lil moment of ecstasy. We reach/ enter utopia (in our minds) where nothing is wrong, and everything is acceptable. We forget that this is temporary and that reality awaits and we continue to go down this road of euphoria like a buffoon; but this shall too pass; we know it, but we're unable to accept it. But when our heart(s) feel(s) 'less lonely', facts present themselves, bursting the bubble of this fond illusion and forcing us to accept reality. And like all the other things in our life, this too elapses and we either run from it (this feeling) or crave it again.

July 2020

Waves crash upon my weary mind,
Rising, falling, cruel, unkind.
I bled my sorrow, let it go,
Buried deep where none shall know.
The land of shadows calls my name,
Yet nothing feels or stays the same.

A hollow space, a quiet ache,
A fleeting past I can't remake.
I wait, I watch, the tide rolls in,
A cycle new, yet worn and thin.
Each wave departs, but leaves a trace,
A whisper lost in time and space.

It's hard, straightening up every time that I fall down
Harder to see myself fall time and again
"this too shall pass"
"You'll find peace at last"
Always preferred being alone
But never felt lonely
Because everyone was around
To console and hold me

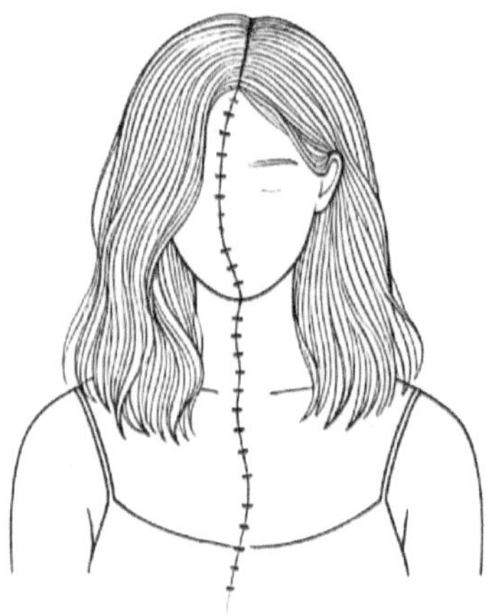

Didn't let anyone in but now I want to
It's always been dark but it's not more serene
"They're just phases they come and go "
Tear me open, a vulnerable prey
Leave me stitched cold and weary

August 2020

I can cease it
Or I can commence
I can give in
Or I can hold out
It's hard to choose
Given my history
But the past is gone
And I've learned my lessons
Am I wiser?
Or still the silly wreck?
Stupid mind doesn't let me feel
Stupid me keeping it concealed
It'll hurt, it's known
I love my 'alone'
Can't jeopardize my mental peace
Shoo away these little beasts
Whispering what is life without heartaches ?
I guess here we go again :p

You're mine
And I'm yours
No labels
Bond is secured
Hurting and hurling
This disease is spreading
Not meant to be
But won't give up
Till it consumes it all
Leaving you hollow
Invested and spent
Only Leading to resentment

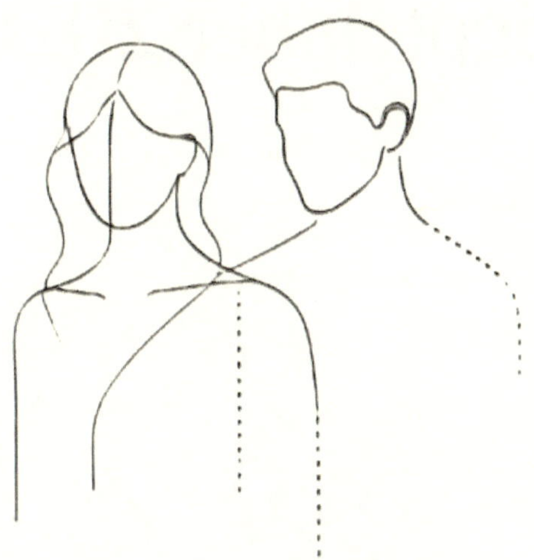

September 2020

You never truly realize how troubled you are until you find a place or a way to ease your tormented soul, only to discover that you can no longer practice it. It hasn't even been a week yet, and I already miss those unintentional moments of contemplation. I miss walking around in those alienated streets, parks, and roads with nothing but the sound of music and the foreign breeze embracing my soul. It was in those moments that I 'felt' content—something that's been so difficult for me lately.

All my confusions would disappear, my worries would feel lighter, and I could finally feel everything I'd been holding back throughout the day. I grew so accustomed to this roaming without care or sitting quietly like a monk, pondering in peace. Now that I know I can't do that, it's truly distressing. I know it's just me overthinking, but I can't wait to go back.

October 2020

Nothing's changed.
The chase remains.
O, the departed soul
Of my paternal love.
The fairest cadaver,
Blue, cold—
A beauty now undone.
Sleeping beloved,
Abandoned here.
The sky, drained of life,
The air, a heavy weight.
Spectators mourn,
At the sight of grace turned to dust.
A heart once pure,
Now shattered,
A strength now feeble,
A presence now hollow.
The body wrapped in cloth,
A final embrace of nothingness,
Left alone,
Buried in darkness,
Forgotten in time.

Draft 2:
Nothing's changed
Same old chase
O the departed soul
Of my paternal love
Prettiest Cadaver
Blue and cold
Sleeping beloved
Left us here
Sky lost its colours
Air so thick
Spectators sobbing
At the site of the beauty deceased
Heart so pure
So dearly relished
Strong stature
Now so feeble
Defunct body Wrapped in nothing but a piece of cloth
Left alone covered in dust in the dark

I'm afraid to face the damage inside.
It gets heavy.
So I break down alone,
masking it with a smile.
Sometimes, it weighs too much.
I can't even let it go.
I carry it,
till it suffocates me.
Until I fall to my knees.
My arms break.
My knees bend.
I taste the ground of my sorrow.
And I lay there,
In sujood

November 2020

Knock, knock.
Who's there?
It's I—
Your crippling fear,
Here to lead you through a dark descent.
Into your insecurities,
Where joy warps into despair,
Euphoria twists into anguish.
You long to scream,
To weep,
But your cries are swallowed by silence,
Lost in an unseen void.
Sorrow falls dry,
Cold, hidden,
Veiled in the depths of your soul.
Close your eyes,
Suffer in your dreams.

Knock, knock.
It's me again.
I'll sew your lips with timidity,
Suffocating you in your own space.
Eyes wide,
Frozen in terror,
Awake, yet lost,
A shadowy presence,
Elusive, yet never near.
Elusive, yet ever near?

this nightmare never ends does it ?...

December 2020

Poetry is not a constant emotion for me; rather, it is a transient amalgamation of thoughts that once inhabited my psyche and corporeal being. If these musings merit contemplation, I transcribe them—an effort to arrest the unrelenting cascade of tragic, chimeric, and predominantly melancholic notions. I find it more facile to articulate my emotions through truncated, disjointed phrases—fleeting expressions that, when synthesized, create the semblance of comprehensive representation, albeit in an obfuscating manner. This process enables me to decipher and relinquish them. As long as I can write, I remain lighthearted and breezy. When I can't, however, it leads to prolonged discomfort. The string of thoughts lengthens, growing until it disrupts my routine and alters my mood.

The beauty of the golden hour in a frame to live forever in my camera roll. Skin glowing, all blemishes that I was unsecured about sparkling like glitters on my skin. The clear blue skies taking all my blues away and radiating my scarred skin making them alluring. I couldn't believe that beauty that was before me in my gallery, was actually me! I clicked multiple pictures and well most of them turned out to be pretty good and I thanked the golden hour for being so merciful and for making me gain my confidence again.

Jan 2021

Stuck in a nightmare
Waiting for it to end
But waiting only makes it worse
Inert body, long breaths
eyes wide open in distress
Clock ticking,
mocking my enervated soul/eyes
Can't do nothing
While everything is scattered
Scattered into a million infinitesimal pieces
hopeless tries in vain

Lips sealed
And hands are tied
By the words of nothingness
And shackles of melancholy
Inanimate legs
Waiting to run away
No matter where I go, what I do
This insidious nothingness follows me around

I solemnly swear,
That I'm up to no good,
The corridors echo,
Where shadows once stood·
The known fills the air,
With whispers that loom,
Revealed in the stillness,
They haunt my alone, a tomb

Feb 2021

Just Many weeks,
few months
Since many months
and a few weeks
Holding on is hard
But letting go is harder
Time, the more I hold on
The more it slips away
How do I hold onto something that isn't there ?
How do I let go of something that's too dear?
Can't accept my fate
Say it : it's never too late
But it is Too late.

April 2021

Here comes the sun once again,
Yet I still feel the weight of this pain.
Blessed with all, yet I still struggle,
In an alien land, lost in a muddle.
Oh, can you hear me, mom and dad?
I'm aching—so much I never had.
You did all you could, gave all your might,
Yet I'm still fighting, even in the light.
I miss your warmth, your tender embrace,
The comfort of home, that sacred place.
God forbid, I feel so far away,
In this strange world, I lose my way.
The sun's here again,
But it doesn't shine the same,
Silent cries of pain,
Trying to stay sane.
Even with everything, I still yearn,
For the love and peace I can't return.

I scrape at the wounds before the scabs can form,
And wonder why the bleeding persists, a quiet storm.
I watch as people tread upon me,
Then wonder why I bruise so easily.
I give relentlessly, even when there's nothing to spare,
And wonder why I'm left incomplete, always laid bare.
With thick skin and layers over my core,
I wonder why I can't feel anymore.

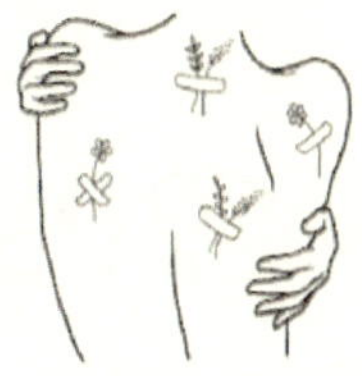

I build walls, high and strong,
Then wonder why nothing ever feels where it belongs.
A puzzle smaller than the labyrinth inside,
I wonder why one missing piece unravels my mind.
I place others before myself,
Then wonder why their expectations rise, overwhelming my health.
Being the same, inside and out,
Comes at a cost so profound,

May 2021

Autumn whispered on an August night,
Back in '09, fading light.
Two children, eight and eleven,
Waiting for their father, a gift from heaven.
They slept, hearts full, dreaming bright,
Woke to storms, love's cruel fight.
From gold to copper, we fell,
Is this how we learn life's spell?
Dark days, colder nights,
No soul, no light in sight.

Months passed since love declined,
Paternal warmth left behind.
Thugs came to steal, life torn,
Twelve sent away, hearts worn.
Nine, ill, swallowing pills,
Innocence lost to bitter thrills.
Degraded by those who once begged,
Now the ones who left them in dread.
Twelve, dissociated, broken, vile,
Fifteen, controlling, lost in denial.
Living in routines, hearts in fright

Fourteen and seventeen, bound tight,
Living in routines, hearts in fright.
In between, they wrote of dreams,
Hoping for better, or so it seemed.
At last, the return, grand and slow,
But five more years, shadows grow.
The story lingers, never undone,
A chase eternal, under the sun.

It's hard to deny what's right in front of your eyes, but it's even harder to accept that the 'worst-case scenario' has become reality. Over the six years of separation, I wrote countless cards, letters, and notes to my father. To know that he'll never get to hold them, never see the words I poured from my heart, still brings a deep ache. It was a strange and painful experience—living with reality yet refusing to believe it, pretending it was all a falsehood. It's terrifying how everything can shift in just one night. People who once filled our home with hollow blessings, who laughed with us only to get what they wanted from him, now feel like ghosts. Family, friends, enemies, well-wishers—all asleep, indifferent, while we bled.

We endured what I wouldn't wish on anyone, not even my worst enemy. The battle was long, for those six years came with an additional five, and they gave others the chance to desecrate our space. After six plus five, it's finally over—almost. Just a few papers left, delayed by this cruel pandemic. But even as time passes, those six years replay endlessly in my mind, and the thought of it happening again terrifies me. It's hard for me to share this, to open this part of myself to anyone. But I need to let it out, even if it's fragmented, even if the words don't fully capture the weight of it.

July 2021

Raindrops cascade, like fleeting thoughts,
Racing to the abyss where silence rots.
Which shall plunge first, with fated grace?
The inevitable, the forsaken, lost in space.
Thunder's fury, the wind's cold sigh,

Erases all in a breath, and leaves no reply.
I fix my gaze on beauty divine,
Suspended in twilight, awaiting the sun's design.
The gentle crash, the murmured plea,
How many souls have it claimed in its spree?

"Paint me any hue but blue," I said,
Yet you cast me in shades of grey instead.
A void, undefined, where clarity lies faint,
A sliver of hope, a scar, a taint.

Never complete, never whole,
An endless fragment, a fractured soul.
Bliss was poured, yet sorrow remained,
Neither pure nor dark, all was strained.

Caught between the poles, torn in the seam,
A state of bewilderment, caught in a dream.
Agathokakology—good and evil intertwined,
A battle unresolved within the mind.

August 2021

Terrorists, militants-whatever they're called-have taken more from me than I could ever express. This isn't just my story; it's the story of everyone who's lost someone to them.

On August 14th, 1998, my father's face was in the paper, hailed as a brave officer who fought off terrorists in Jammu. That same day, these cowards came to my grandfather's house, threatening him that if his son didn't leave the police, they'd make the whole family pay.

Two days later, they returned. My grandfather and his friend were shot more than ten times. He locked my uncle and aunt away, knowing what was coming. When I read the postpartum report, it brought shivers down my spine and my eyes couldn't resist bawling and my heart sunk.

Who will avenge them? Who will remember all the lives stolen by these people?

Every day, my heart aches for the warriors around the world. They risk everything. For what? For us? For justice? But what happens when the cost is too great?

Gloomy greens and eerie nights
Envelope me and take away my frights
Flashy glasses, easily broken
Minds, hardly spoken
Ideal handy simulation preserves
Thoughts clinging to the nerves
Eating up the inside
Fictitious realities hide
Random yet so specific
Keep your finger on the prolific hieroglyphic

September 2021

Pretty faces
Deceptive intent

Many on one
Countless phizogs

December 2021

I am Afshan
20 going strong
From heaven on earth
Idc what you're worth
Don't call me a friend
I don't hop on the trend
Honey sweet psyche
W a huge tendency to bite
I write what I feel
I got no filters to reveal
Strong persona
Spreads faster than corona

When you think it's all good is when it strikes. Sitting in a crowded room, familiar faces seem so alien. Suffocated and confused I turn around to find some air to inhale, but all I get is soot; coughing I fall down; am I dreaming? Is this ecstasy? A voice calls me and I get out of this enchantment; mocking my existence. My unpitying mind loathes itself. Futile junk; can't even sit straight. I grab my purse to take the magic pill; trembling; 1,2,3. :

There's nothing; it's sitting on my table, kilometers away. Not one solicitude figure. What do I hold on to ? Empty eyes staring at each other with poison in hearts. I lay there; in thin air. Forcing myself to smile, sitting in a corner, out walking, doing chores, ... nothing works. Just me and my remorseless self; my casual yet premeditated thoughts envelope my subsistence, my heart pounding in my mouth, and my ears ringing. Sitting and waiting; in a world of ephialtes.

2. There it is; my salvation. Popping. As it dissolves in my body; absorbing every feeling as if I could feel before. Many moments later, it strikes, the nothingness in my nothingness. I'm cured; till it's time again. I smile, unaware yet woke. Body breaking into million pieces; eyes piercing everything around, think! Speak! It's all in my head it's known, yet it isn't.

Jan 2022

Inhaling distress,
Exhaling relief.
Clouds drifting toward the stars,
One touch, disbelief.
Repeated meditations,
Fruity scent in the air.
No conversations,
A foreign feeling, so rare.

Chanting spells,
Pop the magic pill.
Feel it in my cells,
My mind, so still.
Unclear ambiance,
Faint melodies,
Covering the circumference
Of my memories.

Juggling,
The balls catch fire
Balancing,
my hands burning
Not they're ice cold
Sore scars shed tears

Smiling,
Distracting myself from the imminent
Slipping
through my hands
Why don't I feel free ?

Feb 2022

A loud thud. I open my eyes. Above me, stars and moons swirl and rotate in chaotic motion. I can feel my breath, yet it doesn't seem to exist. My limbs are heavy, voices surround me, all speaking at once. It's cold where I lie, yet sweat beads on my skin, my body rigid... I can't move.

I cry for help, but there is no response. I shout, but no sound escapes-only voiceless cries. The rain falls in this claustrophobic space. To my right, to my left, in front, behind-

nothing but voices... noises. I am terrified. What do I do?It's 4 a.m. Where do I go? How do I leave this garden? The cement sky presses down on my chest. The little food I've eaten wrestles in my throat, desperate to escape.

Something grips my throat, tightening, squeezing —slowly suffocating me, just enough to keep me conscious, but every breath is agony. My ribs crack, my chest fractures. I pull the sheet over my exposed body, desperate for some protection. I don't want this. I can't bear it. Everything hurts, yet my mind will not rest.

I thought I had won, fair and square. I gave my blood, my sweat. But it's happening again.

I was just standing there. Outside my body. Looking at me sitting next to the person I'm talking to. The words that were coming out of my mouth, I did not speak them. The hands that moved with the motion of my lips, I did not move them; as I was standing there looking at myself like another person looking at me. The 'me', sitting down, looked around, everything so unreal; no I wasn't high; I didn't take no meds, what's happening?? Why am I so dizzy, why can't I feel my hands ? Why can't I feel what's happening around? Why can't I hear the girl next me properly ? Why does it feel like I'm dreaming or about to dream? I search the room for a familiar feeling but all I got was eerie thoughts. I called my guardian and he read some duas, I relaxed my body and laid down, am I real? Or in a simulation? Am I alive ? Or suffering in my grave ? I don't know. Just scared of the sinister distant yet so near voices; approaching me in full rage; I try to cry but how ?

Which one of us should cry? The one w the sealed mouth looking at the one sitting? Or the one speaking feeling like an alien in her world ?

April 2022

I fear leaving it all behind—the laughter, the tears, the sins, and the scars. This chaotic, overpopulated, and deeply disturbed world feels like home. I fear what lies ahead, the life after this one. But what is life without my loved ones? I could experience every joy and suffering, but without love, I am nothing. It may sound foolish, but I cannot bear the thought of leaving, not yet, not alone.

One day, I will leave, and in that moment, I will witness the cries, the wailing, the tears, while my lifeless body lies on the ground, shrouded in nothing but a white sheet. I will try to offer comfort to my loved ones:

I am here, I am safe, I am at peace...

But they won't hear me, they can't. I will leave it all behind, like everyone else, but sooner than expected. I know this life is fleeting, but its familiarity brings comfort. The unknown terrifies me; I am not ready, and I fear I never will be.

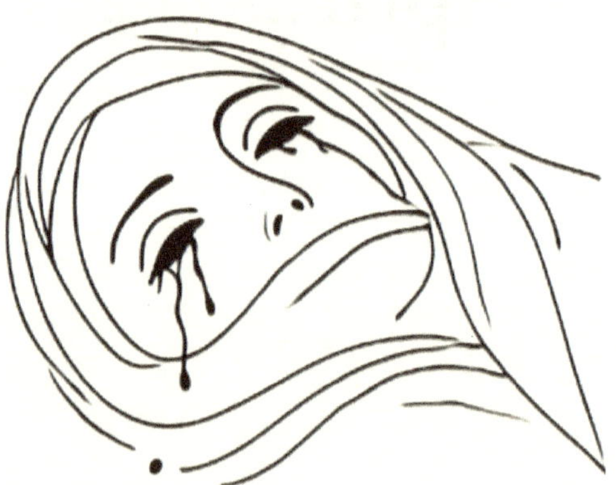

May 2022

This moment arrived as unexpectedly as the last. Yet with each passing embrace, the grip tightens, and with each encounter, new traits emerge or old ones grow more pronounced. I wish they would ask for consent, but they don't. Forcing a smile no longer serves its purpose; they see through the facade, and so the hugs grow stronger. It's chaotic within the core. So many emotions tangled, interwoven. This time, it took me far longer than usual to unravel them, yet they became tangled again in half the time. As each crystal falls away, it leaves behind an entire town in flames—an inferno so uncontrollable that all my defenses can do is envelop me, pulling me away, out of reach, out of reach from myself.

My body is a prison I never chose, It pains to linger here, tethered in this space.
If only I could suspend the moments That stir a desperate need to breathe.

But it's never truly over,
So I release whatever fleeting hope I once held.
I know I deserve the world,
And all the expectations of growing old,

Yet at times,
I yearn to sleep and never awaken.

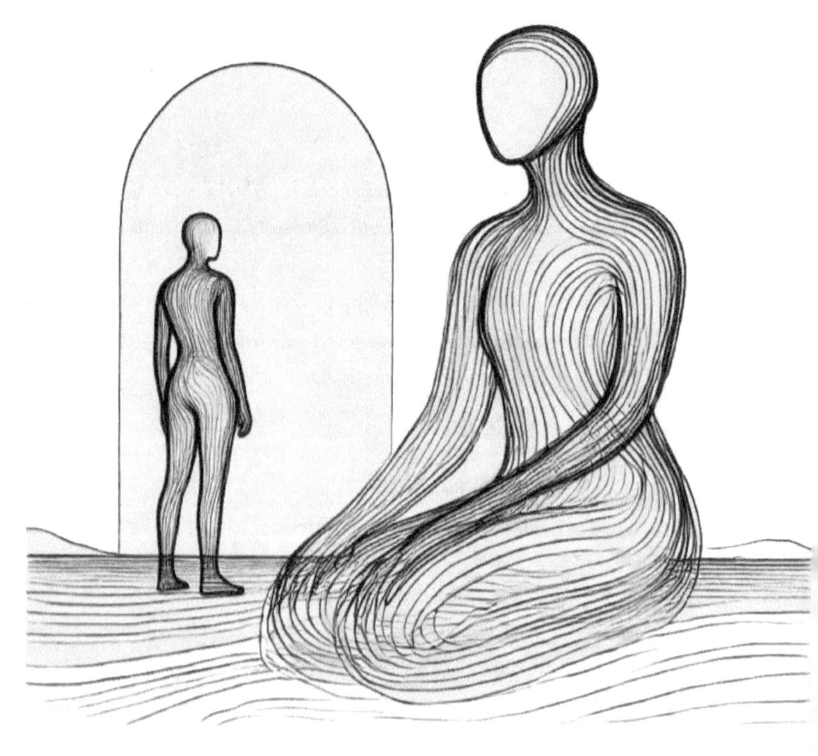

Stitched up a nice silhouette

Masked up merry and might

Replaces me when I'm in the pit

So the world knows nothing of my plight

But whenever I get down to it

It breaks down in fright

So I stay away and quit

Mirrors and sunlight

For its not used to the wit

All it knows is dwelling in twilight

June 2022

In a blink of an eye,
Everything changed
No answer,
Anxiety spiking and tears rolling
Denial took hold
It's not letting go
Many sides of a story
The truth didn't forfeit
The details took me by surprise
Oh! how do I believe that you were right?
Days pass by but I still ponder
Will I ever know what's true?

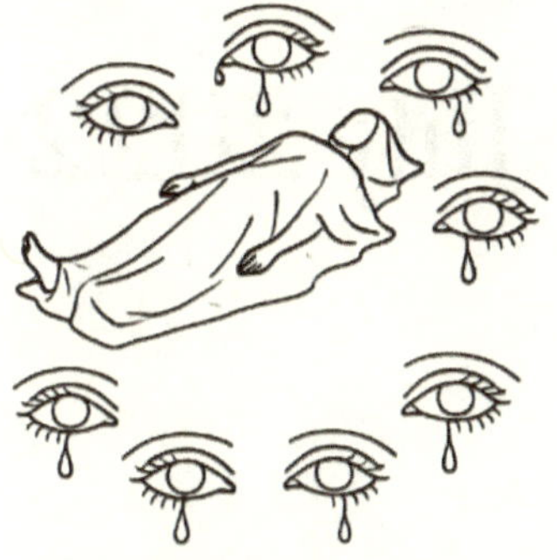

Sooner or later I'll realize
But would it be too late to try?
So I wait
With daggers all over
Too tired to remove or move
I stay still for a rescue..

July 2022

The sky was never 'more blue'
The grass never seemed 'greener'
Pupils never wide enough
Blinded by the butterflies
Moronically leading them to their demise Or maybe desperate to grab
whatever good comes my way

Vision so lucid
Never again will I trip over Threw them pebbles away
Each with a lie engraved
No hate in my heart
Just (another) 'lesson learned' at last.

August 2022

We tend to justify the actions of others out of affection or care. But some actions don't have justifications. We can make up millions of stories in our head for solace, but the relief is only temporary. The lies get slyer and minds more wounded, it's torture. The thing that was once bewitching is now wretched. Nothing can be done to undo what's done but what lies ahead is still in our hands; we either keep sinking or get out of this quicksand.

September 2022

Words stuck like a lump in my throat,
Unable to spit or swallow.
I raise my hand to speak,
But silence binds me tighter,
My voice lost in a storm of hesitation.

Each thought feels heavy,
Crushing beneath the weight of unspoken truths.
I long to scream, to let it out,
Yet all I can do is stand, frozen in the stillness.

October 2022

Blissful wreckage

Shattered and scattered for all to see
What do I do now w this debris?
Senseless intent
Never a friend
I poured and it spilled
Right on the shards, it healed
Picking up one piece at a time
Blood dripping Like slime
Waiting for this tedious errand to be over
Patiently and sober
Solitude in despair
A gift I hear

Laying down on the shards
Consuming my body whole
Prickly little stars
Countless little holes
Skin weeping through the wounds / tears
Each drop dripping ruby
I turn abandoning my fears
Towards the next act, broody

Blissful wreckage pt 2

I look at the person in the mirror often. It's not me I realize from time to time. She's oblivious to all the aches, but there's a melancholy in her eyes, in her smile. It reflects when she smiles, when she speaks, when she smothers herself in the world. The person in the photos, in the videos is someone I am not well acquainted with. She has a glimpse of someone I once knew, adored. I talk to her often and she breaks down; she tells me her predicaments, her hitches, all muddled up. She toughens up in ways I could never.

February 2023

I keep drinking this sweet poison,
A nectar laced with quiet decay,
Seeping through my veins like whispered sins,
Yet stitching the cracks in my soul.

It strips me, scalds me, then makes me anew,
A paradox dressed in velvet ruin,
A lullaby sung by the lips of death—
But tell me, is it peace or surrender?

Abusing prescription,
Leading on,
Chasing silence in bottled storms.

A lull between breaths, a counterfeit calm,
Sinking slow into velvet oblivion.
Is it peace, or just the absence of pain?

March 2023

Greener yet gloomier
You Can't control what is being fed
But you can control what you feed yourself

Things are Never the same even if they're same
Never running out of kindness
I drew a circle to confide the negativity
Now I'm stuck in it

April 2023

I keep putting out the fire I never started
I cup the ocean in my hands,
spilling waves over embers that never burned.
Smoke rises like a ghost of blame,
whispers of a crime I never knew.
Barefoot on the ashes of another's fear,
I chase the wind that fans the lie.

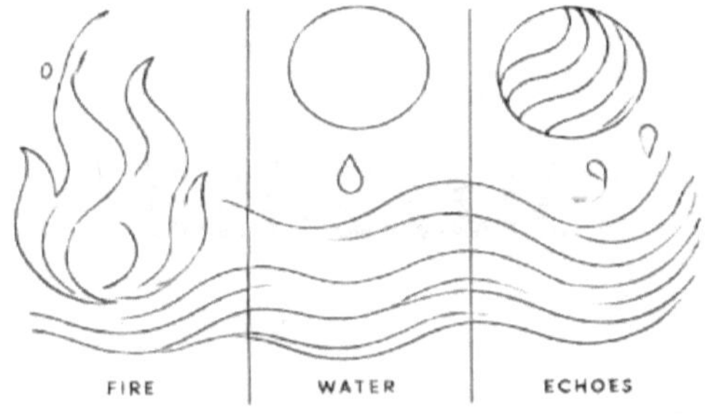

Dousing shadows, drowning echoes,
taming flames that were never mine.
And still, they hand me water,
tell me to fight the phantom glow.
But how do you quench a fire
that only lives in someone's mind?

May 2023

Pick me assorted daisies
Watch me cerebrate
Melange beauty
2 flowers in one
The eminent
to divert the aliens
From the centre eye,
concealed and unsung
Yellow yet always seem blue
Entry restricted

Sit besides me
Watch me daydream
One name so many faces
Each wondrous and adorned with simplicity and purity
Counting these petals with me
Wish we could live in this moment of ecstasy

The sparkle in my eyes
exchanging looks, holding your gaze
Singing the unsung
Moment of divinity
Earthly odor and some stinking slacks
Cloaking desolation

Bring me a daisy
Watch me wonder
As I decipher my soul
And cloak my insecurities
Syrupy moment of affinity
Captivate my vulnerability

October 2023

There's a constant ache in my chest
A constant heaviness
Like all the air has been sucked out of my lungs
And all that's there is a void

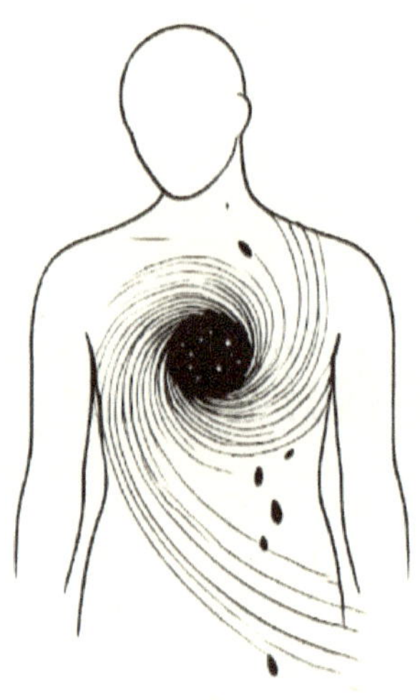

A black hole that sucks everything that I feel
Perplexed by the enormity of this state
I sink in this nothingness
Making peace with: nothing lasts forever

Dim the lights
facing the wretched Thoughts
budding on woeful garden of ecstasy
Waiting to be encountered
Plucking them immature
So that they don't harm more than what I can bear

piercing into my skin
Bleeding tears of abyss
Absorbed by the barren ground
Breeding, more to come
Absolute solidarity
Blooming all ceaselessly
Cold spectrum

Is our perception a true reflection

or

a distorted image of reality?

NOVEMBER 2023

Regret turned into poetry
But when did melancholy turn into ecstasy?

I don't want to be a part of any race. I just want to be, to exist, and to pass. Slowly dive in the sea and experience it all, rather than dragging myself/rushing to the finish line. I want to be at peace. Swim at my pace, observing and feeling everything; immensely.

Love is a shapeshifter, a quiet trick of the mind, woven from fleeting moments and chemical sparks that dance in the brain.

It isn't just romance or grand gestures——

it lingers in the simplest acts, in the spaces between words It's the way a child clings to their parent's hand, the way a mother feeds her child without question, the way a dog's tail wags with unfiltered joy at the sight of home.

It's the unspoken comfort of returning to someone who melts the weight of the world off your shoulders. It's a brother who bickers endlessly, yet without a word, orders your favorite things when you're too worn to ask. Love is everywhere, scattered in the quiet corners of existence, not just in the people we choose, but in the moments we never expect.

December 2023

Here I am again

A scared lil girl peeping from the crack on the door

Listening to everyone shouting your name

Trying to wake you up

But you weren't there

Just a lifeless vessel

all blue and cold

I don't remember when I lost it

Crying on the praying mat

Or when I cracked and started laughing w the neighbours while running away from them

Or when I prayed that it was me instead of you

I was 8

Years drift like autumn leaves,
day by day, hour by hour,
yet the ache remains unfading, unyielding.
With each soul that departs,
something within me crumbles,
a silent ruin in the wake of absence.
How am I unshaken in all but this
a fortress against the world, yet a phantom before fate?
I do not know if I am here,
or merely a whisper in the hollow of my own mind.

I have made peace with it,
but is surrender a triumph or a quiet defeat?
If only time would fold upon itself,
fast-forwarding to the hour where I am whole again,
where I walk among my beloveds,
leaving behind those who will soon follow
guiding them in dreams,
offering the solace I cannot now.
Would they hear me then,
in the hush of the wind,
in the hush of their hearts?

March 2024

Growing up, I struggled with numerous insecurities and lacked confidence in myself. Although I was never bullied, I always had this nagging feeling that people were mocking me. Even compliments felt disingenuous, and discovering that some people spoke ill of me behind my back only intensified my self-hatred.

I had natural wavy/curly hair which I obviously resented, so I resorted to straightening them every day and using all sorts of hair creams and serums to 'fix' them. Witnessing others' bodies undergo significant changes during puberty while mine remained relatively unchanged further fueled my insecurities.

It took considerable time for me to embrace and accept myself for who I am, reaching a point where others' opinions about my appearance hold little sway, as long as I feel good about myself and maintain my well-being.

Now I do the things that I want to do, without the fear of judgement because you're not important enough for me to take anything you say seriously. As long as I'm not harming anyone with my actions, I don't really care about how they're perceived by anyone.

Comparing oneself to others is of no use since we all have our own uniqueness that we should learn to accept and embrace. No one's ugly we just need a little grooming and confidence. Remember, you are stunning just the way you are!

I fled with the wind at my back,
feet chasing shadows, heart packed with dust,
seeking a place where silence spoke,
where walls would welcome, where love would trust.
Through cities bright and forests dim,
over bridges burned, through rivers wide,

each door I knocked on whispered "stay,"
yet none could hold the storm inside.
The farther I went, the less I found,
each road a circle, each sky the same.
I sought a home that never was,
only to learn-I had no name.

The wave comes crashing. It's getting unpredictable over time. When does it end? That's all I think. Why this time? That's irrelevant. 'It'll pass. It'll pass.' I try to calm myself. The gushes of cold water wash away all the past progresses; the world I built; which was never mine to begin with.

The mania has faded and the emptiness begins. I pop one it doesn't work, two I'm dizzy, three I get nightmares. I puff one, it fades, two fades again, three it hits a little, four five six and the whole pack is gone. But I still feel the same.

I count my breaths as I disappear in the bubble of solitude; oh my lovely solitude; where it's just me in my bubble. The mind works in mysterious ways doesn't it?

I imagine something unearthly filling the buckets and taking out the water; it smiles; it soothes; but I still feel alone. It's comforting now. To be alone. To not be a burden.

It gets worse; and worse; but I don't lose hope do I? I never do. Why don't I end it all? Ik why. I'm not ready to face the almighty. What do I show him? What did I do? Sins? But he'll understand won't he? That I tried and tried.

The anchor is too strong. It won't let the ship topple I know. The ship won't topple until it's time and I don't decide the time.

April 2024

I have learned: through fire,
through ache,
that love without borders is a costly mistake.

Give without thought, and they'll take without end,
never once asking if you need to mend.

So I build my walls, not out of stone,
but out of wisdom that pain has sown.

Boundaries,
lines: etched deep, defined,
not to keep love out, but to guard what's mine.

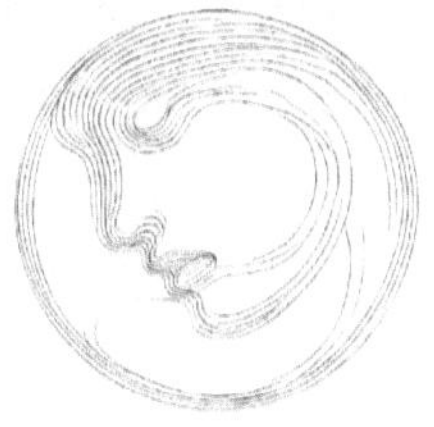

No soul deserves the whole of me,
save the One who breathed me free.

For this world is cruel, a thief of light,
draining hearts in the dead of night.

Yet even in shadows, joys remain,
small flickers of warmth to soften the pain.

And I will find them, hold them near,
without letting my past cloud what is clear.

For I am not here to break, to bend,
nor to make my wounds another's end.

But to live, to heal, to stand, to see:
and give only what is safe in me.

May 2024

Laying on the cold cotton sheets,
head sinking in the soft pillow
W eyes closed my blanket hugs me, tugging me tightly
Rubbing my feet against each other
As the cool summer night breeze brushes my hair, kisses my cheeks
I hear the Clock ticking
The tree branches whistling
The cars gliding on the road
My breathing becomes deeper
Heartbeat slower
I descend into my dreams

June 2024

A question that often crosses my mind
Am I or am I not?
Cessation of existence
Mania sets in
Dilated and elevated
Energetic and dissociated
From the pretty sunset to the pretty moon
My journey is completed
Now all that is done and dusted
All that's left are
imprints for me to visit

Look closely for you may find
Corpses
wrapped in these Creaseless folds of shallowness
Dumped
in the brown pills of despair
Adorned
w roses, peonies and carnations

Lit up
w faith and hope
Read for you may see
It's all written all over this phiz
That my yearnings tend to cease
Once only thorns are left to exist

They say the storm must break before the sky can clear,
but why does it tighten its grip, pulling me near?
I have known pain: flesh torn, bones weak,
but nothing compares to the ache that doesn't speak.

Wounds of the body, they mend with time,
but the mind: oh, the mind: is a slow-burning crime.
A fever breaks, a scar will fade, yet these ghosts remain,
these debts unpaid.

I ran from the place that first made me small,
from walls that whispered, from shadows that call.
But even from miles away, they creep,
curling through dreams, dragging me deep.

And still, they expect me to turn around,
to retrace my steps, to kneel, to be bound.
But if I go back, I know I will break:
not softly, not gently, but in fire and quake.

So I run, though the road twists tight,
choking my breath, swallowing light.
Better the weight of a world unknown
than the hands of the past that once made me stone.

Visiting the catacombs
Deserted by mind but held by the soul
I see versions of myself spread across
Skulls of what
Once was
and what could've been
The uncertainty that
Once was
The certainty
I now crave
I visit it often to learn
But the learning turns into yearning and I stay there for a
while
I'm afraid one day I might never return.

It's strange how little a person becomes

Once you see them for who they're and not for what you made them in your mind.

I believe it didn't take you much to clear out the ideal image of you I had in my head

and to slap me

Back to reality to find

That you were nothing

It's strange because I don't miss you,

I don't think about what Once was,

I don't see you

Even in my past rather the present or the future

It's a blessing or a curse Idk but all I know is

That you're nothing

It's strange how content I'm w your absence.

I don't have a single nice memory to hold onto because it was in my head,

Never true

That's why it never made sense

Not one word you say holds value or hurts or has any influence

Because for me there's only one reality that's true and that's

That you'll always be nothing.

July 2024

I have had this question many times in my head: what is love? And I think I finally found the answer.

It's a polymorphous state of mind backed by chemical reactions in the brain which are released only when someone you tend of adore (because they're your relative / they did something for you which no one else did/ they made you feel a certain way that one time) is near.

It is all around us;

I feel it when I see a child hold his parents' hands while waking. When a parent feeds their child. When a dog wiggles its tail when he sees his owner. When after having a hard day you come home to someone who just takes your worries away. When your brother who always fights w you sees you in pain and orders your favorite things without asking.

I often pondered how it would end,
these smoldering desires, too jagged to mend.
The epiphany struck as I met your gaze,
a whisper of warnings, a labyrinth of haze.
Wayward choices carve paths to despair,
yet truth be told, I'm still ensnared.
I keep my distance, resist the sway,
but molten ice melts my resolve away.

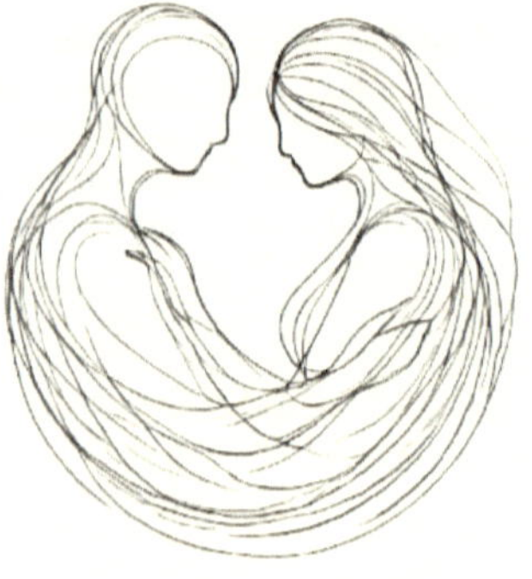

For I had caged it in frost for years,
now it quickens—no snow, just fears.
Lips like nectar, your touch divine,
arms that cradle and soothe what's mine.
A shelter I never dared to seek,
you lift my doubts, make my insecurities weak.
Recklessly, I played the cards I dealt,
but in your embrace, a new strength is felt.

The hands that once brimmed with strength,
Now bear the weight of fleeting years,
Wrinkled, freckled, they whisper tales,
Of time that slips and disappears.
The snack box, once a trove of cheer,
Now holds the solace of pills, not treats,
Where laughter once echoed, bright and clear,
Now silence sighs in quiet beats.
The crooked smile, once wild and free,
Now fragile, worn by countless days,
And eyes that sparkled with unchained glee,
Are veiled in sorrow, lost in haze.
The man who once lifted me high,
Now stands, a shadow, faint and frail,
The woman who ran to feed my cry,
Now stumbles, her steps slow, pale.
Timid trails of time unwind,
In every wrinkle, every line,
A love that once was fierce and wild,
Now whispers softly, sweet and kind

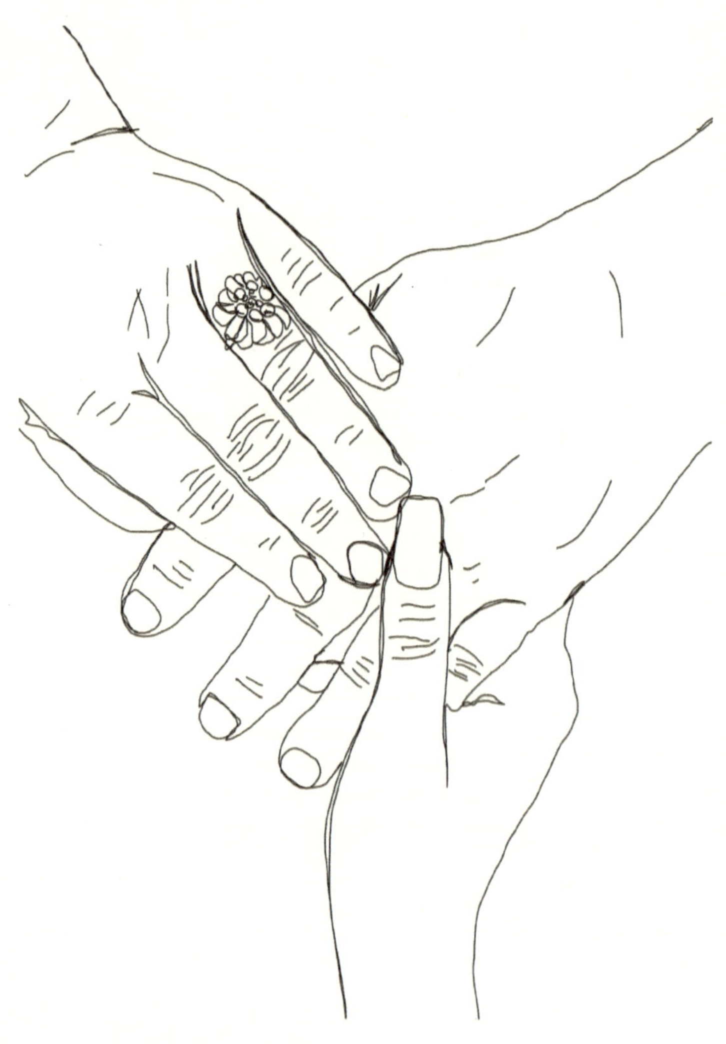

August 2024

I'm good w the pen I say

As I sit in front of the blank canvas glaring blankly at my half witted mind

Senseless and agitated
For again,
no words seem to formulate,
no lines, no strokes can defined what I feel;
how I feel inside

But I've always been good w the pen I say

W years rolling down my cheeks, hands trembling, my heart beating in my chest
This heaviness is consuming my being;

I don't recognise the person standing in front of the mirror,
Holding the pen; engraving ' I'm here' ' I'm here' on the glass

As the blood seeps through the shards
Oh! The mess I've made

But haven't I always been good w my pen?

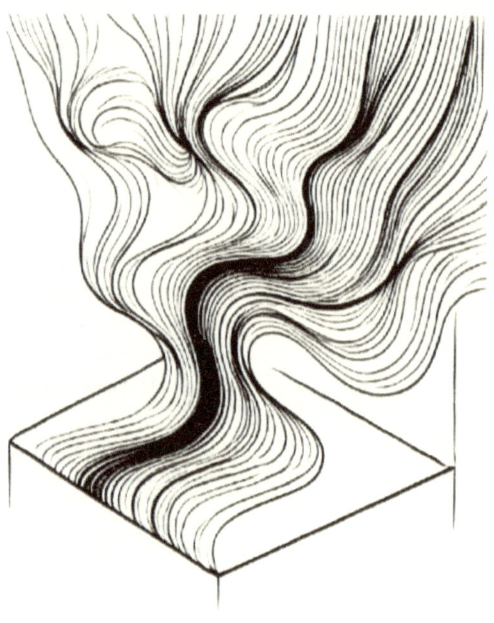

I'm not my past but the lessons I learnt along the way. I'm a collection of versions
that Once was and the ones I'm yet to become making homes for the new ones on the
graves of the old ones
The graveyard is my home.

October 2024

Maybe in another universe you're not worlds apart;
But next to me, holding the tea cup Pouring the tea,
listening to our favorite band on repeat;
Maybe the sun shines a little softer,
While we dance and sip our evening tea;

There's laughter echoing in our eyes,
Our hearts filled with nothing w peace;
Maybe we're dealt w the right cards,
With Feelings flourishing and thoughts caged,
Listening to the symphonies of our souls singing in
unison.

November 2024

You don't really understand the meaning of love until you've had a furry friend by your side. One who knows nothing but you, who grows up thinking you're their entire world. They're only part of your life, but you are all of theirs.

Loki was there when I needed him the most. His little paws on my chest, his purring against my heart, wiping away my tears with his face. Every time I broke, he knew. He'd come running, make me sit, and ground me with his quiet presence.

To others, he may have been "just a cat," but to me, he was more family than most of my relatives. Even when he was unwell, he comforted me. I do remember my old times, when I was sick and hospitalised and none of my family showed up. But my Loki, always by my side, even when he was on his deathbed, he held my hand, rubbed his face against my tears and made sure I didn't cry while he was going through his treatment. He passed away in my arms, looking into my eyes with those golden ones I'll never forget. My beautiful boy. I love you. This next page is for him.

My Beautiful Boy
In loving memory of Loki

They say you don't truly understand the depth of love
until you've known it in the silence of a heartbeat,
wrapped in fur,
with eyes that speak without words.

You were never just a cat.
You were the rhythm my world fell into
when everything else was noise.
You knew only me
and somehow, that knowing was enough
to tether me to the earth
when I felt like drifting away.

You grew up watching me break
and somehow pieced me back together
with the gentle press of your paws on my chest,
with purrs that hummed against my ribs
like lullabies made of starlight and breath.

Your golden eyes held galaxies,
but they only ever looked for me.
Each time the storm rolled in,
you felt it before I did.
You'd come running
no hesitation, no judgment
just the soft insistence of your presence,
demanding I sit,
be still,
and let you love me back to life.

Some say it's too much,
this ache I carry for an animal.
Your little body curled beside mine,
even when yours was weakening.

Even in your final hours,
you tried to comfort me.
You wiped my tears with your furred cheeks,
rubbed your fading face into my hands
as if to say
"Don't cry, I'm still here. I'll always be here."

You took your last breath in my arms,
eyes gleaming one last time

and in that moment,
I knew what unconditional love was.
Not in words, not in promises
but in presence, in touch,
in the quiet goodbye of a soul saying thank you.

This page is for you, my golden-eyed guardian.
For the warmth you gave,
for the nights you made bearable,
for the parts of me you helped keep alive.

I'll carry you always.
In poems.
In memories.
In the still corners of my chest
where your purrs still echo.

A small incision Peeling off the dermis
Laying down layer by layer The layers of my being
Spread across on a vast land
Everything that I'm made of

Blood gushing out As I scream and splash
My organs all around Till nothing is left that hurts
It's painful yet comforting

My known hell
Grass all red, I cease to exist
Terrified I continue, because it's the easier way out

December 2024

The light within me, a flicker that persists,
Guides me to places I can't quite exist.
It feels so foreign, yet it won't release,
A pull I can't escape, a whisper of peace.
Why does it linger, when all is askew?
So distant, so strange—yet still it feels true.
Why won't it fade, this thought in my mind?
More vivid than sight, it's all intertwined.
What am I clinging to in the depths of this haze?
The warmth, the echo, the pull that betrays.
It wasn't all sweet, yet why does it stay?
Why am I lost in a memory's sway?
I've had more than this, haven't I?
A future untangled, a star in the sky.
But here I am, caught in this place:
Stagnant, awaiting a dream I can't chase.
What's this obsession that gnaws at my soul?
A need for something, though I don't know the whole.
What will it take to break this spell?
Is it obsession: or a longing to quell
Right?
Or is it just more than I see?

I leave fragments of myself in every soul I meet,
Whispers of my essence, soft and bittersweet.
If our paths crossed, if our hearts aligned,
No matter where you wander, I'll linger in your mind.
A trace, a spark, a piece left behind,
Carried with you, woven through time.

In every word, in every glance,
I live on, within the dance.
So wherever you go, whatever you do,
You'll find a part of me: forever with you.
A fleeting touch, yet eternal, true:
I am in you, and you in me too.
I like to leave pieces of me in people I meet
If we ever connected, No matter what you do where you go, you'll carry me with you

EPILOGUE

The first step to healing is acceptance, and through this release, 1 have embraced my younger self with nothing but love. 1 hope you do too. We are who we are today because of everything we've been through; good or bad. And while, for some of us, the bad may have outweighed the good, 1 promise you this: nothing lasts forever.

Healing begins when we accept ourselves as we are, acknowledge our past without resistance, and move forward with a clear and open heart. It's not an easy journey, and 1 know how exhausting it can be to go through it alone. But you're not alone.

There's something my dearest cousin once told me that has stayed with me, and 1 want to share it with you in the hope that it helps: Surrender. When 1 told her 1 already had—that 1 was going with the flow—she stopped me and said, "There's a difference between giving up and surrendering. Imagine you're on a boat in a river. You can either stop paddling and cry about being stuck, or you can keep rowing in the direction of the current and find a way forward. The former is giving up, which leads to nowhere—it will only make you lose balance and fall. The latter is surrender. If you can't go against the flow, move with it. Keep paddling, save yourself, and you'll find your way."

Seeking the help you deserve and choosing to heal is the greatest act of love you can give yourself. Because at the end of the day, it's you who has to carry your struggles—not society, not even your parents or friends. You. And whenever you feel alone, 1 want you to come back to these words and remember—you're not.

Take these lines and make them your own. From my heart to yours.

ACKNOWLEDGEMENT

(Eternalized with words)

I have so much to be grateful for—Alhamdulillah! But today, I want to take a moment to thank some very special people who have stood by me through everything.

My parents — You set aside your traditional views to see the world through my eyes, creating a safe space for me to explore myself, my thoughts, and my soul. Thank you for spoiling me endlessly and for trying your best to adapt and grow with me.

My brother — Even with your own struggles, you always put me first, and I can't tell you how much that means to me. I'm so grateful that we've finally become friends.

My family (most of you!) — Thank you for giving me a space where I could express myself freely and for loving me unconditionally since childhood, and for never letting me outgrow my childlike wonder and whimsy. (I've seen my childhood pictures—I was not a pretty sight. Alhamdulillah for puberty!)

My friends — You've seen me go through countless phases, yet you've chosen to stay. You are my chosen family. Thank you for always being there for me and not letting me lose my mind over my book; and for always helping me out with your insights and honest opinions.
My shers : I love you and I'm glad to have you in my life.

Special thanks to:
    Saltea studio- For their insights and marketing
    Notion Press — For helping my words reach the world.
    (Saransh — For handling this process so well and guiding me through it.)
    Pragya — For your insights & for connections—your degree definitely came in handy!

I couldn't have done this without you.